My Little Brother has Hirschsprung Disease

Eric and Isabelle Schnadig

Illustrations by

Isabelle Schnadig

My Little Brother Has Hirschsprung Disease, Published November, 2020

Editorial and proofreading services: Beth Raps, Karen Grennan
Interior layout and cover design: Howard Johnson
Interior and cover illustrations: © Isabelle Schnadig

Photo Credits: Family photo owned by Schnadig Family

Published by SDP Publishing, an imprint of SDP Publishing Solutions, LLC.

ISBN-13 (print): 978-1-7343317-7-6
ISBN-13 (ebook): 978-1-7343317-8-3

Printed in the United States of America

To Claire, Paul, Nathalie, and their little brother Adrien, with everlasting love.

ACKNOWLEDGMENTS

WHEN OUR SON ADRIEN WAS BORN 14 YEARS AGO, we searched high and low for information about Hirschsprung disease. There wasn't much available, Today, we are fortunate that the quality and quantity of resources have improved. Nonetheless, no children's book tailored to the needs of the Hirschsprung community exists. We wrote this book to fill that gap.

We are pleased to publish the book under the auspices of REACHirschsprung's, Inc, the official name of the not-for-profit that we founded 11 years ago—"REACH" for short.

We are grateful to the many people who help the Hirschsprung community meet the challenge of this disease. Thank you surgeons, researchers, other medical professionals, and caregivers! You help heal the sick, discover new treatments, and share best practices to meet the needs of our community.

Thank you to all of the parents and families who take care of children with HD. Coping with this disease is no small matter. It is very impactful to have a community that shares daily challenges, achievements, pains, and joys.

Thank you also to the REACH Board! We are blessed to have found each other and to work with such an intelligent, dedicated, and kind group of parents and professionals.

Finally, we thank our wonderful families and friends. You make our mission possible and give it purpose and meaning. We love you.

ABOUT HIRSCHSPRUNG DISEASE (HD)

HD AFFECTS APPROXIMATELY 1 IN 5,000 BIRTHS, accounting for over 850 new cases yearly in the U.S. and 26,000 worldwide. HD is caused by the absence of *ganglion cells* in the colon which results in the inability to poop normally. Hirschsprung disease takes its name from Harald Hirschsprung, a 19th century Danish pathologist who described the condition in patients.

When undiagnosed and untreated, the disease causes belly distension, constipation, and *enterocolitis,* leading to life-threatening illness. The severity of HD is typically related to the length of the colon affected, with short-segment patients suffering a less severe form of the disease than total colonic patients, whose entire colons lack nerve cells. When diagnosed early and correctly, kids with HD develop and live well.

To help readers understand the medical terminology associated with HD, there is a brief glossary on page 25 of this book. Words in italics in the book are included in the Glossary.

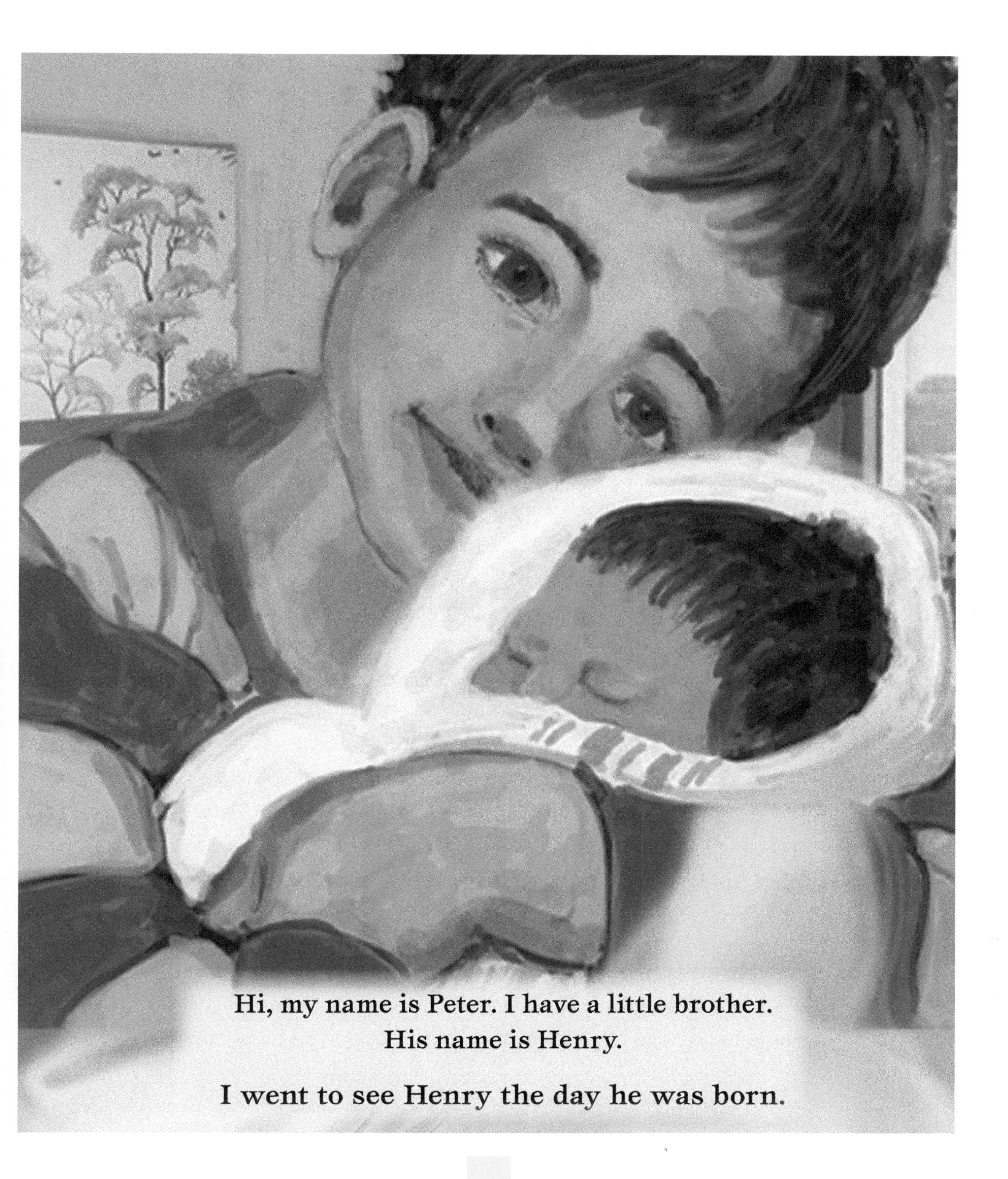

Hi, my name is Peter. I have a little brother.
His name is Henry.

I went to see Henry the day he was born.

After two days in the hospital, Henry got very sick and started throwing up. His tummy got very big. The doctor said he could not pass his first poop. The doctor called it the *meconium* (muh-CO-nee-um).

The doctor said Henry had to go to another hospital, in Boston. My mom and dad went with Henry in an ambulance. I was worried about Henry.

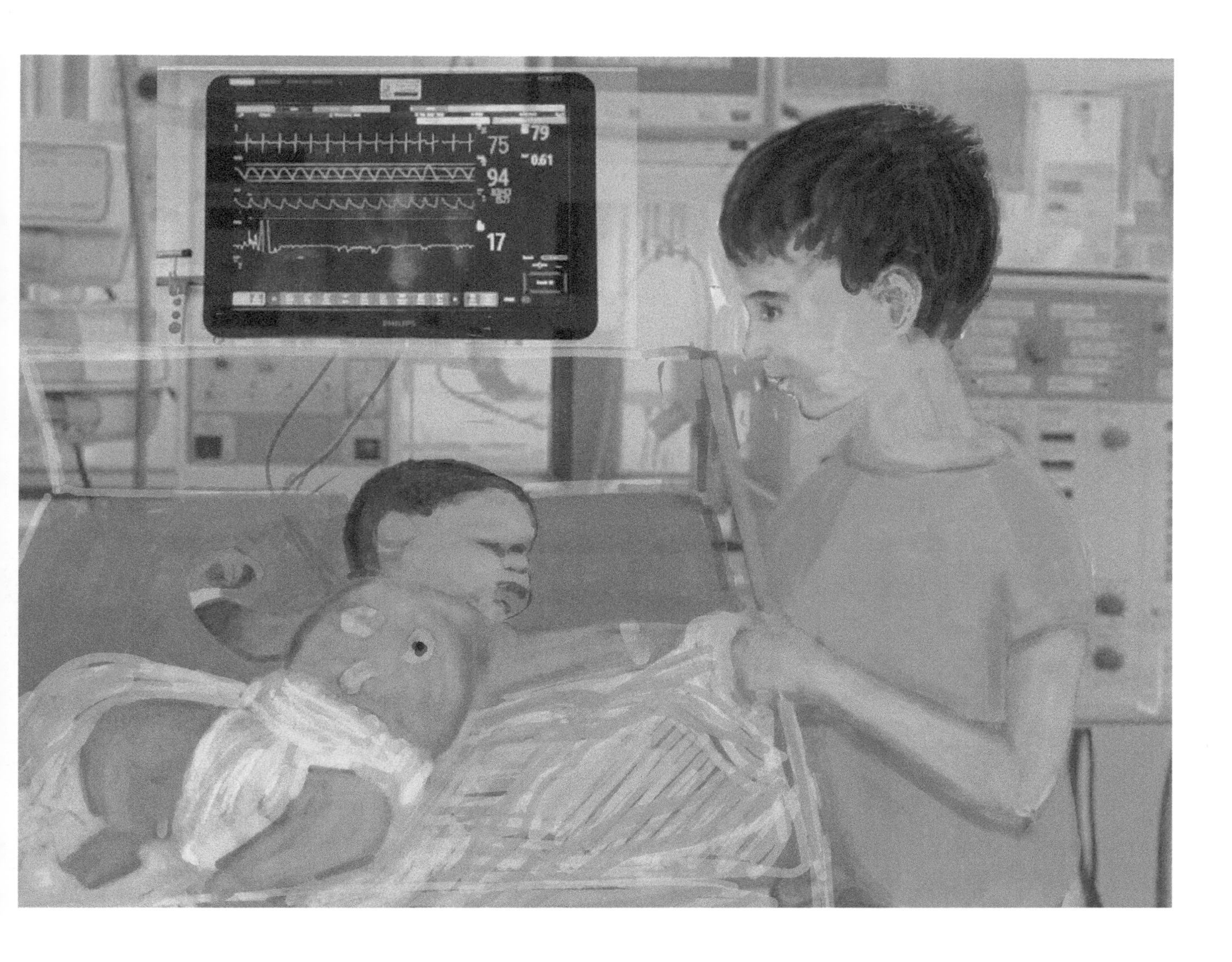

I went to visit Henry at the bigger hospital. He was in a special place called a NICU. I learned that NICU stands for “Neonatal Intensive Care Unit.” It’s a special place for sick babies where they get extra attention from doctors and nurses.

I had to wash my hands every time I went to visit Henry. When I saw him, he had wires attached to him and there were machines all around.

Henry's new doctors did some special tests to find out why he wasn't pooping. They did an x-ray of his belly and then they did a *biopsy* (BI-op-see) of his *rectum*. The next day, his doctor told us he had Hirschsprung disease. They call it "HD" for short.

The doctor explained that Henry's *colon* (COLE-un) was not working right. His colon couldn't squeeze and relax like mine can, so no poop was coming out.

Henry was missing nerve cells in his colon. The doctor told us that those nerve cells are called *ganglion* (GANG-lee-on) cells.

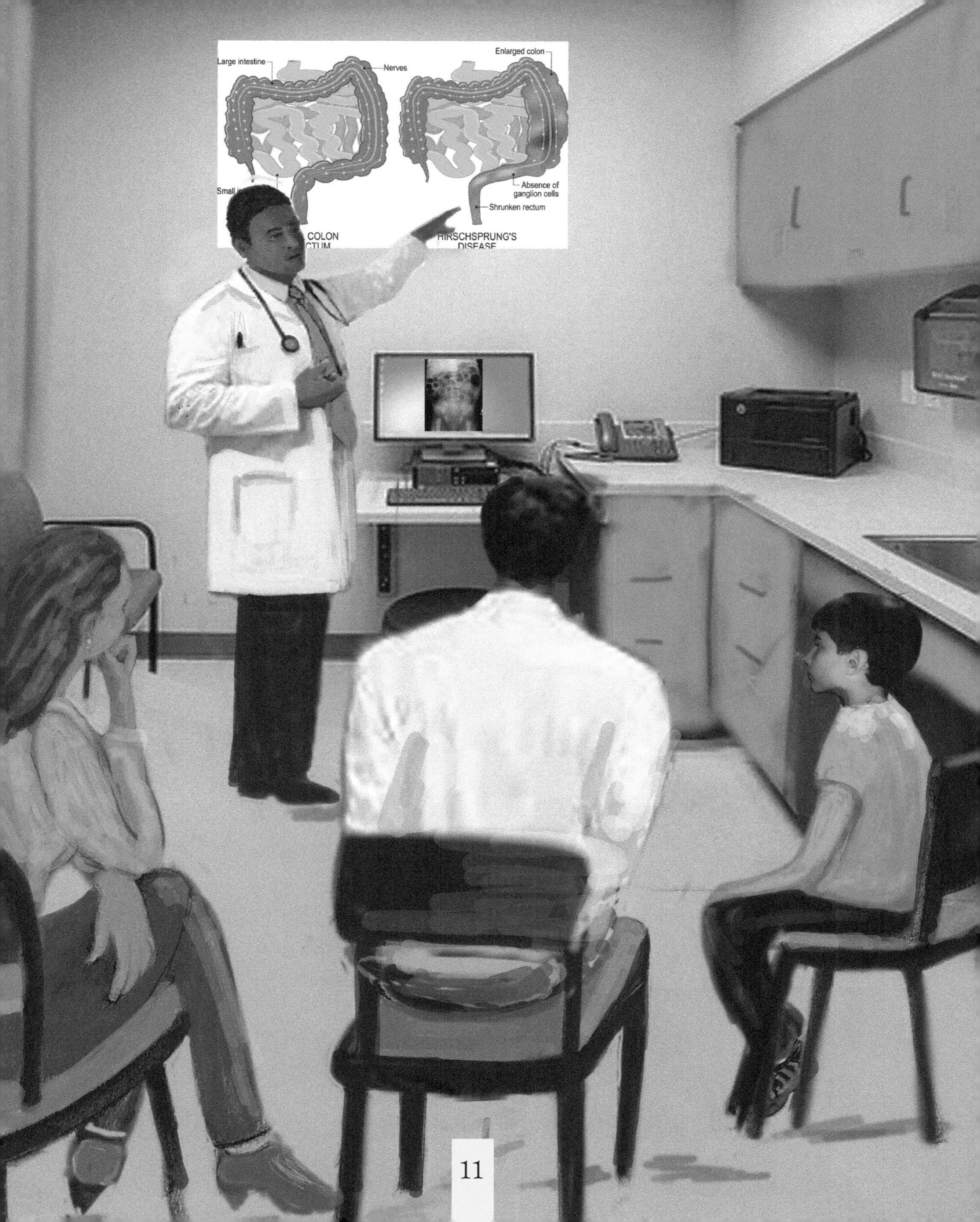
Large intestine
Nerves
Enlarged colon
Absence of ganglion cells
Shrunken rectum
COLON
HIRSCHSPRUNG'S DISEASE

Henry needed surgery to help him. The doctor explained that when it was all done, my baby brother would have a big bandage on his stomach. Plus, he would have a little bag attached. They called it an *ileostomy* bag (il-ly-OSS-tum-me). Henry needed that because he had no nerve cells in his whole colon!

My mommy and daddy showed me how to change the bag. I remember seeing it for the first time—it was pretty weird but really cool!

It was great to be back home with Mom and Dad and my new baby brother. He was fun to play with! But I had to be careful about the bag for a little while. If it came off by accident, it made a mess and smelled bad!

When Henry was 20 months old, he went back to the hospital for another surgery. This time the doctors attached Henry's healthy intestine to his rectum, so he could poop like all of us. The doctors were waiting for Henry to be bigger and stronger for this surgery and he was finally ready. The surgery was called a "pull through." It went really well, and my baby brother now has a big scar on his tummy.

Now Henry spends a lot of time on his little potty learning how to poop. Mom and Dad make a big deal each time he goes. We even started a family poopy dance! My friends think that's pretty funny.

Sometimes, I feel like my parents are always thinking about Henry. ***Has Henry gone to the bathroom? Is Henry sick? Is Henry eating enough? Is Henry sleeping enough?***

Sometimes I get mad. When I tell my parents, they agree that it’s hard and I feel better after I get a big family hug. I also like when I get to spend time together with just me and my parents.

Henry is doing better, but he gets sick when he eats certain foods. The doctors say he has food *allergies,* so we have to pay attention to what we eat around him. Also, Henry has to drink a lot every day. If he doesn't, he gets dehydrated. That's because he is missing his colon.

Here's another thing about Henry. Whenever he gets sick, it takes longer for him to get better, especially when he gets a tummy bug. My parents say the best medicine is more handwashing.

There are lots of fun things we get to do with Henry. I like the summer when we go to new places together. Sometimes we get to take an airplane to visit family. That's great because we all love airports and airplanes.

We've noticed that Henry doesn't do well in hot, dry places like the desert. The best places for Henry are warm and humid near the water. Wherever we go, my parents always remember to pack extra medical supplies for Henry.

Nowadays, most of the time, my parents can take care of Henry without doctors and hospitals. If he's having a hard time pooping, first we try belly *massage*. That helps him pass gas.

We like to call it "bad gas" and we all laugh. Sometimes "bad gas" happens outside our house, like at the movie theatre. When that happens, it can be a little embarrassing.

When Henry can't pass gas or poop, my parents give him an *irrigation*. That helps clean out the poop when he can't push it out by himself. Henry always feels better after an irrigation.

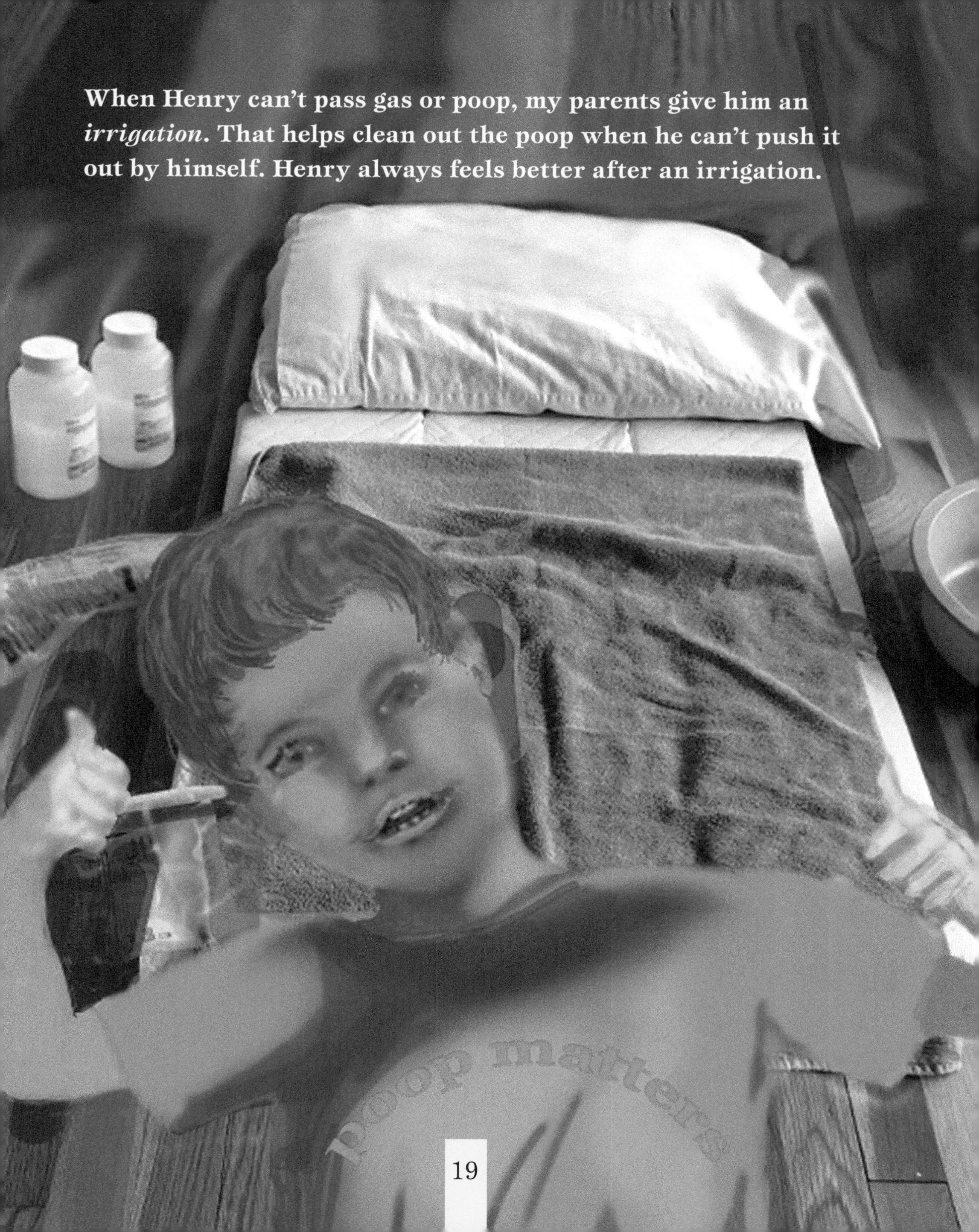

Today, Henry is 9 years old and he is doing much better. Sometimes we even forget he has Hirschsprung disease! Henry is a good swimmer. We have a blast snorkeling together.

But there are other times that it's hard to forget he has HD, like when he has to wear a pull-up at school. His teachers know that he has a special condition, but sometimes the kids can be mean, like when they tease Henry.

When that happens, Henry feels sad and hurt. We talk about it together. Henry likes my idea of making a presentation to his class about HD. And after my parents talk to Henry's teacher, we all agree to help Henry get ready.

When I am older, I want to be a scientist to find a cure for Hirschsprung disease.

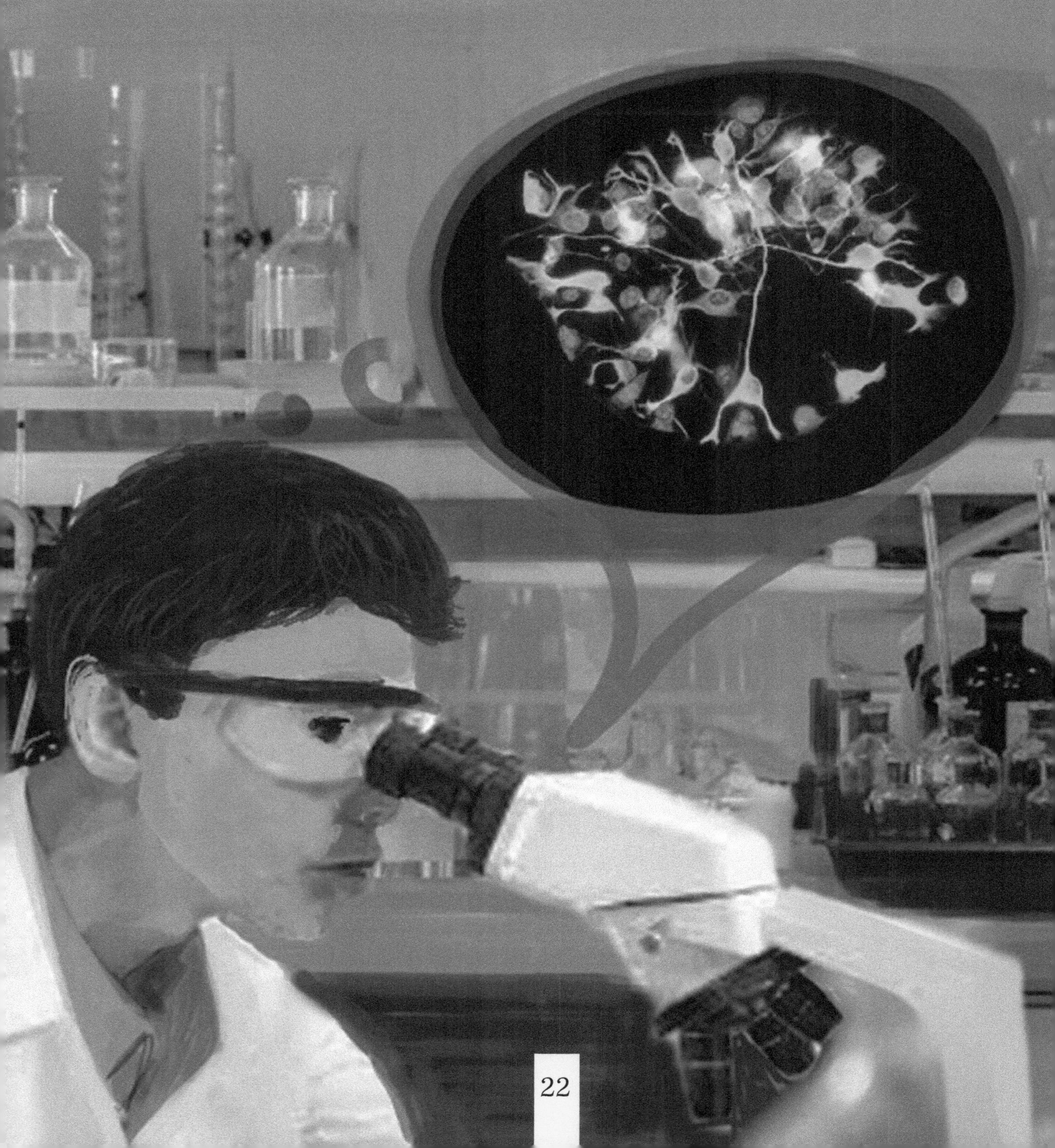

In the meantime, my parents say that we can all help out in different ways. I'm going to raise money and awareness for HD by running in a race in my town.

GLOSSARY

ALLERGIES: A damaging response by the body to an external substance, typically pollen, animal fur, particular foods, or dust, to which the body has become hypersensitive. A large number of people suffering from HD have food allergies. The interrelationship between food allergies and the disease is not well understood.

BIOPSY: An examination of tissue removed from a living body to discover the presence, cause, or extent of a disease.

COLON: The main part of the large intestine that absorbs water and electrolytes from food that has remained undigested. (The parts of the colon are called the ascending, transverse, descending, and sigmoid colon.)

ENTEROCOLITIS: Inflammation in a person's digestive tract that affects the small intestine and colon. While enterocolitis can happen to anyone, it is a particular risk to people with HD. It causes fever, abdominal swelling, and nausea, and when undetected or untreated can be life-threatening.

GANGLION CELLS: Also known as a nerve cell. In the bowel, these control contraction and relaxation and allow for normal bowel movements (pooping).

HIRSCHSPRUNG DISEASE: A disease of the large intestine where the ganglion cells are absent, preventing the normal function of the bowel and resulting in the inability to poop normally.

ILEOSTOMY: An operation in which a piece of the small intestine (called the *ileum*) is diverted to an artificial opening in the abdominal wall.

IRRIGATION: Washing out the bowel with water or medication. For HD patients, the process involves using a catheter tube and saline solution to remove excess gas and stool from the bowel.

MASSAGE: Rubbing and kneading muscles and joints with the hands, especially to relieve tension or pain. Stomach massage alleviates gas pains for HD patients.

MECONIUM: The dark green substance forming the first feces of a newborn infant.

RECTUM: The final section of the large intestine, terminating at the anus.

MORE ABOUT REACH

REACH stands for **R**ESEARCH, **E**DUCATION, and **A**WARENESS, for **C**HILDREN with **H**IRSCHSPRUNG Disease. It is a not-for-profit organization founded in 2011 by parents and physicians committed to improving the lives of children and families with Hirschsprung disease. If you would like to learn more or help, please contact us at: reachirschsprungs@gmail.com and follow us on Facebook at www.facebook.com/reachhd/ and Instagram at www.instagram.com/reach_hd/.

Our website is *www.reachhd.org.*

ABOUT THE AUTHORS

Eric and **Isabelle Schnadig** are a husband and wife book-writing and illustrating team. They are also the proud parents of four wonderful children: Claire, Paul, Nathalie, and Adrien, and are co-founders of **REACH**, a not-for-profit dedicated to research, education, and awareness for patients and families with Hirschsprung disease. They work and live in Concord, Massachusetts.

CPSIA information can be obtained
at www.ICGtesting.com
Printed in the USA
JSHW010339300321
13039JS00001B/1

9 781734 331776